65p

Chippendale

Edward T Joy

COUNTRY LIFE COLLECTORS' GUIDES

Secretary in satinwood inlaid with various woods. About 1770–1775. Attributed to Chippendale on stylistic grounds. Collection of the Earl of Harewood, Harewood House, Yorkshire.

Chippendale's Career

Numbers in the margin refer to the page where an illustration may be found

Thomas Chippendale (1718–1779) is without doubt the most famous name in the history of English furniture, perhaps the best known name in world furniture. No study of the Georgian period, that famous 'golden age' of English craftsmanship, could possibly be complete without paying special attention to his contribution to cabinetmaking, which is now fully accepted as part of England's cultural heritage. The reasons for this eminence are clear enough. His identified pieces of furniture include outstanding examples of craftsmanship and design, worthy of holding their own with the finest work of foreign masters, even with that of the celebrated French ébénistes who, until the outbreak of the French Revolution in 1789, were regarded as Europe's best craftsmen. Chippendale was also the first man to publish a **pattern book** which was completely devoted to furniture designs, including every type of domestic furniture, down to the simplest pieces. The success of this book – the *Director* of 1754 – established his reputation and subsequent fame and attached his name to the mid century style which, though French in origin, was given by him an unmistakable English character and which has become the first English furniture style to be named after a craftsman and not after the reigning monarch. English furniture was widely imitated in many European countries at that time, as well as, of course, in the English colonies, and the label 'Chippendale' has now gained universal acceptance as a convenient description of pieces in the *Director* style. Since Chippendale's career outlasted

4

THE
GENTLEMAN
AND
CABINET-MAKER's
DIRECTOR.

BEING A LARGE

COLLECTION
OF THE MOST

Elegant and Useful Designs of Houshold Furniture

IN THE

GOTHIC, CHINESE and MODERN TASTE:

Including a great VARIETY of

BOOK-CASES for LIBRARIES or Private ROOMS. COMMODES, LIBRARY and WRITING-TABLES, BUROES, BREAKFAST-TABLES, DRESSING and CHINA-TABLES, CHINA-CASES, HANGING-SHELVES,	TEA-CHESTS, TRAYS, FIRE-SCREENS, CHAIRS, SETTEES, SOPHA'S, BEDS, PRESSES and CLOATHS-CHESTS, PIER-GLASS SCONCES, SLAB FRAMES, BRACKETS, CANDLE-STANDS, CLOCK-CASES, FRETS,

AND OTHER

ORNAMENTS.

TO WHICH IS PREFIXED,

A Short EXPLANATION of the Five ORDERS of ARCHITECTURE, and RULES of PERSPECTIVE;

WITH

Proper DIRECTIONS for executing the most difficult Pieces, the Mouldings being exhibited at large, and the Dimensions of each DESIGN specified:

THE WHOLE COMPREHENDED IN

One Hundred and Sixty COPPER-PLATES, neatly Engraved,

Calculated to improve and refine the present TASTE, and suited to the Fancy and Circumstances of Persons in all Degrees of Life.

Dulcique animos novitate tenebo. OVID.
Ludentis speciem dabit & torquebitur. HOR.

BY

THOMAS CHIPPENDALE,
Of St. MARTIN's-LANE, CABINET-MAKER.

LONDON.

Printed for the AUTHOR, and sold at his House in St. MARTIN's-LANE. MDCCLIV. Also by T. OSBORNE, Bookseller, in Gray's-Inn; H. PIERS, Bookseller, in Holborn; R. SAYER, Printseller, in Fleetstreet; J. SWAN, near Northumberland-House, in the Strand. At EDINBURGH, by Messrs. HAMILTON and BALFOUR: And at DUBLIN, by Mr. JOHN SMITH, on the Blind-Quay.

opposite
Title page
of the first
edition of
the *Director*
(1754).

the *Director* period, and since by general consent his best work was produced in the succeeding Neo-classical era in what has become known as the Adam style, his achievements in this later phase, in which he employed quite different materials and decorative methods, is a further tribute to his remarkable skill and versatility.

These are the foundations of Chippendale's reputation, firmly based on clear evidence. But it is important to remember that there is relatively little documentary material about his life and nothing on his vital early years. He himself left no journal or diary or autobiographical data. Plenty of his drawings have survived, but these, while invaluable for stylistic study, convey little or nothing of his life story. Practically the sum of contemporary material on which we have to rely for our knowledge of his career consists of evidence such as the entries in parish records of his baptism, marriage and burial and in rate books of his various addresses; very occasional newspaper references; some letters to and from clients; bills for executed commissions; and passing references to him in diaries, notebooks, etc. But research into his career continues unceasingly, and more and more information, even if only fragmentary, is coming to light. Certainly much more is known about him now than ten years ago, most of it, it may be added, enhancing his reputation.

With so many gaps in our knowledge, it is essential to put Chippendale's career into proper perspective, for hero-worship can encourage both exaggeration and denigration. Until quite recently, for example, it was assumed that all good pieces of English furniture in the *Director* style must have come from Chippendale's workshop. But apart from the obvious fact that no single shop could have produced so much furniture, it is now also known that his fame has unfairly obscured, until recently, the worth of highly gifted contemporary cabinetmakers, particularly those who succeeded in obtaining what Chippendale never achieved – a royal appointment. In 1768 Chippendale claimed in a letter to Sir Rowland Winn at Nostell Priory, Yorkshire, that he was busy with work 'for the Royal Family', but there is no reference to him either in the royal household accounts preserved in the Lord Chamberlain's archives at the Public Record Office, or in the official papers at Windsor Castle. These contemporaries were all capable of producing work of superb quality, some of it directly based on the designs in the *Director*, which was after all intended to be a trade guide. It is also obvious that, once he had set up in a fashionable London shop, Chippendale himself could never have made any furniture. He was principally a designer, and this task, together with that of running a busy shop, and of travelling to attend to clients' commissions in all parts of the country, would inevitably have taken up all his time. There is still relatively little furniture that can be unequivocally assigned to Chippendale's workshop, though the number of identified pieces is increasing as more evidence appears. The methods of identification and attribution of Chippendale furniture, as well as the known number of his commissions, will be examined in more detail later (page 36).

Barometer of tulipwood and ebony, supplied by Chippendale to Nostell Priory in 1769 for £25. Collection of Lord St Oswald, Nostell Priory, Yorkshire.

Mahogany settee, based on a design for a French chair (Plate XXII) in the *Director* (1762). Metropolitan Museum of Art, New York (Harris Brisbane Dick Fund, 1957). (See 20)

Chippendale's career may be outlined briefly as follows. He came of Yorkshire stock, the son of a joiner in the small town of Otley, where he was baptised in the parish church on 5th June 1718. Between this date, recorded in the parish register, and 19th May 1748, when he married Catherine Redshaw at St George's chapel, Hyde Park, London, there is a complete blank. What happened in these thirty years, the most formative in any craftsman's life, is matter for pure speculation. Nothing is known of his training, of when he moved to London, or of his first job there. It has been suggested that local Yorkshire patrons, recognising the young man's promise, sponsored his journey to London to complete his training, and the Lascelles family, of nearby Harewood, and Sir Rowland Winn have been mentioned in this connection. Another suggestion, made more recently, is that James Paine, the architect, met Chippendale at Nostell Priory where he was working as a joiner (and where he is said to have made the fine doll's house which is still there) and recommended him to study drawing at the St Martin's Lane Academy, founded by Hogarth in 1735, where Paine himself had studied. This Academy, in the heart of London's fashionable cabinetmaking world, may well have been an important training ground for furniture designers, but more research is required before the exact nature of its influence can be judged.

Mahogany urn stand on double scroll legs. About 1760. Temple Newsam House, Leeds.

Rate books reveal that Chippendale was living in Conduit Court, Long Acre, from 1749 to the summer of 1752, then in Somerset (or Northumberland) Court, Strand, next to Northumberland House, from 1752 to 1753, and finally, by 1754, at 60 and 61 St Martin's Lane, where he remained for the rest of his life. A wall-plaque, where St Martin's Lane meets Long Acre, now marks the site of the workshop of England's most famous cabinetmaker.

Chippendale had evidently acquired, in his early thirties, sufficient capital and prestige to find himself among the most eminent furniture-makers of his day. In 1754 he took a partner, James Rannie, a further indication of expanding business, and

Part of the Sun Fire Office's policy register for 1755 recording Chippendale's policy covering his premises in St Martin's Lane, London, against fire. The total value of the property, including separate amounts for glass, wearing apparel, utensils and stock in trade, was £3700, and the annual premium was £7 9s. The extract reads: 'Thomas Chippindale of St. Martin's Lane in the Parish of St. Martin in the Fields & James Rannie of   Cabinetmakers and upholsterers On the now Dwelling house of the Said Thomas Chippindale Situate as aforesaid with a warehouse behind adjoining and Communicating On the Right Hand Side of the yard not Exceeding Eight Hundred pounds . . . £800'. Guildhall Museum, London (on loan from the Sun Alliance & London Insurance Group).

in the same year became nationally known through the publication of the *Director*. A fire at his premises in 1755 was reported as having destroyed the 'benches of 22 workmen'. In 1760 he was elected a member of the Royal Society of Arts on the recommendation of the Yorkshire landowner, Sir Thomas Robinson of Rokeby Hall. In 1766, on the death of Rannie, Chippendale held a sale of his stock-in-trade, which was announced in the *Public Advertiser*. In 1771 he acquired another partner, Thomas Haig, formerly Rannie's clerk. Meanwhile, he visited France in 1768, and perhaps as a result of arrangements made during this visit,

Set of standing shelves, japanned, formerly at Badminton House, Gloucestershire. Lady Lever Art Gallery, Port Sunlight, Cheshire.

he imported unfinished French furniture, presumably to complete in his workshop, for in 1769 he was fined by the Customs for under-declaring the value of 60 French chair frames. He married a second wife, Elizabeth Davis, in 1777. He died of consumption in 1779 and was buried in St Martin's church. He had altogether eleven children, and his eldest son Thomas (born in 1749) succeeded him in the business and also became a distinguished cabinetmaker.

Chippendale's London was not only by far the largest furniture centre of the British Isles, but was also one of the largest in Europe. The chief English provincial cities – Bristol, York, Norwich, Bath, etc. – had competent craftsmen who were well able to supply local needs, including those of the gentry, but they followed London fashions, for the most eminent cabinetmakers and the finest shops were found in London, nurtured by court patronage and by that of the landed aristocracy who made their seasonal visit to the capital to keep abreast of the latest furniture styles. London-made furniture went to great houses in all parts of the country, as far north as Scotland. It was also exported throughout Europe and the colonies. Through their key trading position London furniture-makers had ready access to the world's finest cabinet woods, above all to mahogany, now available in ever increasing quantities. In every way in furniture-making, the capital's position was unrivalled.

By about 1750 the select group of high class shops maintained by the leading makers had left the once fashionable area of St Paul's Churchyard to group in the district of St Martin's Lane, Long Acre, Covent Garden and the Strand, with extensions, somewhat later in Chippendale's career, into Old and New Bond Street and Tottenham Court Road. It was these shops which catered for the royal family and the aristocracy. Some were of considerable size, though the largest so far identified, that of George Seddon, was in unfashionable Aldersgate Street. This was reported by a German visitor in 1786 to be employing some 400 craftsmen. But most shops must have been much smaller than this. The fashionable furniture world was highly competitive. Successful cabinetmakers had to seek the patronage of influential clients, catch the latest fashion, and select the most skilled journeymen, all while facing heavy overhead expenses (wages, rent and rates, timber stocks, etc.). The nobility were notoriously unpunctual in paying their bills. 'As I receive my rents once a year,' wrote Sir Edward Knatchbull of Mersham-le-Hatch, Kent, to Chippendale in 1771, in reply to the latter's request for payment, 'so I pay my Tradesmen's Bills once a year, which is not reckoned very bad pay as the world goes.' Fashionable cabinetmakers very rarely advertised through trade cards, as this practice was frowned upon by the well-to-do.

Games box supplied by Chippendale to Paxton House for £4 14s. 6d. Collection of Mrs H. Home Robertson, Paxton House, Berwickshire.

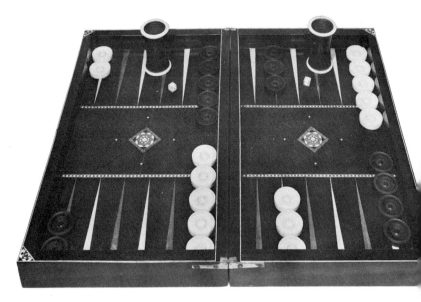

The Director

This was the London into which Chippendale launched in 1754 his *Gentleman and Cabinet-Maker's Director*, with the subtitle 'a large collection of the most Elegant and Useful Designs of Houshold Furniture in the Gothic, Chinese and Modern Taste'. It was dedicated to the Earl of Northumberland. Its impact can be measured by the fact that no furniture pattern book on this scale had ever before appeared in England. Various furniture designs had certainly been published – those of Vredeman de Vries had been imported from Flanders as early as the 16th century – but they had normally been in the form of plates of furniture appended to books on architecture. Now there came on the market a book exclusively concerned with furniture, embracing the three styles then in fashion, including all articles of furniture, and with the addition of decorative details and descriptive technical notes. The title of the book proclaimed its purpose of being a guide for both the discerning patron and the craftsman, 'calculated', as the preface explained, 'to assist the one in the choice and the other in the execution of the Designs'.

Of the three styles of the *Director*, by far the most important was that which Chippendale called the 'Modern Taste' but which today is familiar as the Rococo. This style, which originated in France shortly before 1700, was a deliberate reaction against the massive formal classicism of the Baroque, and was characterised by delicate **C- and S-scrolls**, asymmetrical in form, using shells, flowers, foliage and rocks (whence *rocaille*, the French name for

Carved and gilt mirror, one of a pair, corresponding to a design (Plate CLXXI) in the *Director* (1762). Collection of the Hon. Mrs George Marten, Crichel, Dorset. (See 32)

the style), often combined with amusingly distorted human figures, birds and animals, especially monkeys. In France the style began with the arabesque designs of Jean Berain and Pierre Lepautre; then followed, about 1730, the *genre pittoresque* or mature phase created by the engraved designs of Nicolas Pineau, the Turin decorator J. A. Meissonier, and others. In England the Rococo began to make ground when it was on the wane in France. After 1748, the year of the death of William Kent, the fashionable architect who designed Palladian exteriors and rich Baroque interiors, the way was open for a change of taste. Several small pattern books by Matthias Lock and Henry Copland had already included designs in Rococo taste for carvers and artists, their furniture being mainly confined to drawings of mirrors, console tables and picture frames, all carvers' pieces. In 1753 *The Analysis of Beauty* by the artist, William Hogarth, had come out decisively in support of the supreme beauty of the 'serpentine line or line of grace', and it says a great deal for Chippendale's business acumen that he seized the moment so admirably to apply the style to all kinds of furniture while carefully controlling it so as to suit English traditions and to avoid exaggerated versions. This is the true Chippendale or *Director* style.

The subordinate Chinese and Gothic styles of the *Director* further underlined Chippendale's acute sense of opportunity. Interest in chinoiseries had revived after the translation into English in 1736 of the great travel book on the Empire of China by the Frenchman, Du Halde. Pattern books of Chinese designs had been published in England in the early 1750s by Matthew Darly and W. and J. Halfpenny, and in some large houses it became fashionable to have a Chinese room, complete with imported, hand-painted Chinese wallpaper, and with furniture made in England to match the decoration. Though this Chinese taste was based on many misconceptions, and indeed came in for much contemporary ridicule, it nevertheless provided craftsmen with a kind of escape route into a world of fantasy, and many charming articles resulted. What has now become familiar as 'Chinese Chippendale' contained two contrasting elements:
21 geometrical fret- or latticework ('**Chinese railings**'), and scroll-

work incorporating **oriental motifs** such as pagodas, bulrushes, mandarins, long-necked birds, bells, etc., all of which blended smoothly with the prevailing Rococo and were perhaps best typified in the magnificent gilt mirror frames of the time.

Chippendale's **Gothic**, unlike the other two *Director* styles, was English in origin. It was inseparably connected with Horace Walpole who in 1747 bought his famous house at Strawberry Hill and began to transform it into a Gothic villa. Walpole gave Gothic a very personal interpretation. The interior was decorated with delicate Gothic tracery copied from famous examples of medieval work, and the furniture to fit into this scheme had pointed arches, arcading, finials and crockets. 'Strawberry Hill Gothic' was later derided as a frippery, bastard version of the original, but in the 1750s its dainty filigree ornament merged easily into the intricate curves of the developed Rococo style.

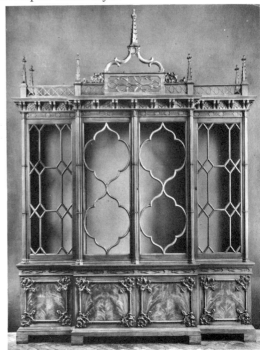

Mahogany bookcase based on a design (Plate CI) in the *Director* (1762). Lady Lever Art Gallery, Port Sunlight, Cheshire.

It is probable that at least two years were spent on the preparation of the *Director*. It was published in 1754 at the high price of £2 8s. and contained an imposing list of 310 subscribers who were presumably circularised beforehand for their patronage. They were in two main groups, craftsmen and well-to-do patrons. Most of the former came from the various furniture trades—carvers, upholsterers, joiners, cabinetmakers, etc., and included some well known names—Gillow, Seddon, Ince, Parran, the Channons, etc. Among the well-to-do subscribers was a good sprinkling of dukes, earls, barons and baronets.

The *Director* had a second (practically unchanged) edition in 1755 and a third (enlarged) in 1762, when the price was raised to £3. The first and second editions contained 161 plates, dated 1753 and 1754, all signed by Chippendale ('T. Chippendale invt. et del.') and mostly engraved by Matthew Darly, with a few by T. & J. S. Muller. For the third edition, only 95 of these plates were retained, and 105 new ones added, all again with Chippendale's signature. Chippendale's own responsibility for the designs has been questioned. In 1929 it was maintained by Fiske Kimball and Edna Donnell of the Metropolitan Museum, New York (in 'The Creators of the Chippendale Style' in *Metropolitan Museum Studies*) that he had employed two commercial artists, Lock and Copland (mentioned on page 15) as his 'ghosts' on the *Director* designs, Copland being responsible for the designs of carvers' pieces. There certainly seems to have been some relationship between Lock, the pioneer of the Rococo in England, and Chippendale, for drawings by both men are found together in various surviving collections, and as Lock did not publish anything between 1740 and 1769, he may well have been in Chippendale's employment during that period. On the other hand, Chippendale signed all the plates, and in the preface he states that he himself was the author—'I frankly confess that in executing many of the drawings, my pencil has but faintly copied out those images that my fancy suggested.' There seems to be no reason to doubt his word. Close examination of both the Lock and Chippendale drawings by experts has convinced them that Chippendale must be given complete credit for his designs. The evidence in favour of Copland's responsibility is particularly unconvincing. Moreover, evidence has recently come to light (it is examined in detail on page 53), making it abundantly clear that Chippendale undertook most of his own designing in which he showed remarkable ability and originality.

The enlarged third edition of the *Director*, reflecting Rococo taste at its height before it was swept away by Neo-classicism, provides the best basis for study of the Chippendale style. It shows the diversity of furniture to be found in the better class of mid Georgian households. There were also relatively cheap pieces intended for more ordinary homes. Chairs and other seats had 25 plates to a total of 60 designs, of which 24, entitled 'chairs' or 'chairbacks' were in the anglicised version of the Rococo. Added to these were French, Chinese, Gothic, ribbon back ('ribband back'), hall and garden chairs. The typical Chippendale

19 **Rococo chair** has become one of the most famous of all chair designs, with its 'cupid's bow' top rail, uprights which curve gently outwards, and its interlaced, pierced splat of light and

19 fanciful scrolls and curves. **'Ribband back' chairs** were extravagant versions of this taste and only three designs for these were included in the *Director*. They were no doubt intended for the more zealous devotees of French fashions. Rococo chair designs were sometimes shown with two different front legs. This gave them a strange appearance, but was done, as the text explained, 'for the greater choice' of prospective customers. The front legs were either straight or of graceful cabriole form. In the latter case the claw-and-ball foot, which had been fashionable since about 1710, was no longer used, but was usually replaced by a scroll, which turned either outwards ('French scroll') or inwards ('knurl foot'). For chairs with straight legs stretchers were reintroduced after being out of fashion for half a century (they had been discarded once the cabriole leg had established itself in Queen Anne's reign). This reappearance of stretchers raises an interesting question of design, for they were not really necessary from the structural point of view, particularly now that mahogany, with its almost metallic strength, was available. For the upholstery of these chairs, Chippendale recommended

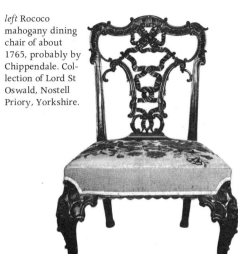

left Rococo mahogany dining chair of about 1765, probably by Chippendale. Collection of Lord St Oswald, Nostell Priory, Yorkshire.

below 'Ribband Back Chairs'. Plate XV, *Director* (1762).

above Mahogany 'ribband back' chair. About 1755. Victoria and Albert Museum, London.

Ribband Back Chairs.

S.ᵉ Chippendale inv.ᵗ et del.   Publish'd according to Act of Parliam.ᵗ   M. Darly Sculp.

that 'the Seats look best when stuffed over the Rails and have a Brass Border neatly chased; but are most commonly done with Brass Nails, in one or two Rows.' Rococo chairs certainly had a charming elegance and lightness of line which made a startling contrast with the heavy chairs of the Kent period.

20, 21   The so-called 'French' chairs were upholstered armchairs. Two of these had plain backs, but the eight others had carved and scrolled frames, arm supports and seat rails, as well as slender cabriole legs. The notes in the *Director* stated that some of these chairs were 'intended to be open below at the Back; which makes them very light, without having a bad Effect'. Light indeed they were, the phrase 'open below at the Back' indicating that they were to have a space between the back and the seat rail. As their name implies, such chairs were modelled directly on contemporary French chairs, and many of them were gilded.

21   'Chinese' chairs had their backs filled with latticework and had either a straight or curved top rail. One design showed a pagoda cresting. These chairs always had straight front legs which could be left plain or else decorated with pierced or low relief frets. Such decorated legs had a fret-cut bracket at the angle with

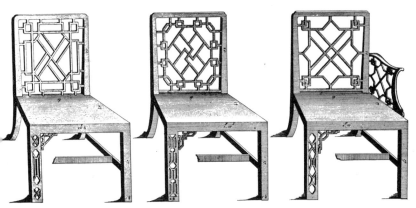

above 'Chinese Chairs.' Plate XXVI, *Director* (1762). (See left)

left Mahogany chair in Chinese taste, based on a design (Plate XXVI) in the *Director* (1762). Victoria and Albert Museum, London. (See above)

opposite 'French Chairs.' Plate XXII, *Director* (1762). (See right)

right Armchair in carved mahogany, based on a design (Plate XXII) in the *Director* (1762). (See opposite)

the seat rail which sometimes also had low relief carving. Sometimes, too, the side and cross stretchers had pierced frets. Bedrooms were considered particularly suitable for Chinese decoration, and Chippendale's notes state that his Chinese chairs 'are very proper for a Lady's Dressing-Room; especially if it is hung with India Paper...They have commonly Cane-Bottoms, with loose Cushions; but, if required, may have stuffed Seats and Brass Nails.'

'French Commode Table.' Plate LXV, *Director* (1762). (See below)

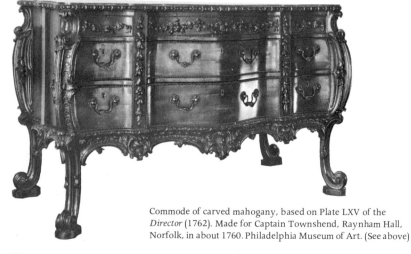

Commode of carved mahogany, based on Plate LXV of the *Director* (1762). Made for Captain Townshend, Raynham Hall, Norfolk, in about 1760. Philadelphia Museum of Art. (See above)

A 'Gothick' hall chair with open Gothic patterns in the back was not one of Chippendale's happiest designs as it was far from capturing the delicacy of Strawberry Hill tracery. But many of the interlaced Rococo chair backs incorporated attractive Gothic motifs such as ogee arches, trefoils, quatrefoils, etc. Of the other seat furniture of the *Director* mention may be made of sofas (which had continuous upholstered back and sides) and couches (which had only one end raised). With one exception the designs showed versions of cabriole legs and, further proof of French inspiration, the rails were curved and decorated with Rococo motifs.

22   The most fashionable of all pieces of furniture at the time, regarded almost as a status symbol, was the **commode**, the ornamental chest of drawers which stood in the most prominent position in the best room of the house. The 'French Commode Tables', as they were called in the *Director*, showed every refinement of form and decoration – serpentine fronts, Rococo carving on frieze, apron piece, end supports and cupboard doors, and ornate gilt handles.

Japanned commode formerly in the Chinese Bedroom, Badminton House, Gloucestershire. Probably supplied by Linnell about 1754. Victoria and Albert Museum, London.

Commodes were made with drawers either extending the full width across or placed centrally and flanked by cupboards; or else the whole front was enclosed. Some were **japanned**, as they were intended to stand in bedrooms decorated in the Chinese taste.

As a general rule, the *Director* designs for tables in Rococo style had cabriole legs, while those in Gothic and Chinese taste had straight legs, with the further distinction that Chinese tables had fretwork carving on their frieze and legs. The Kent period had been distinguished for its monumental side tables with marble tops—'immeasurably ponderous', as Horace Walpole had rightly described them—and these now gradually went out of fashion once the *Director* style had established itself. But some of these 'sideboard tables', though of smaller proportions and of more restrained decoration, were still apparently intended to have marble tops, for only in one instance (Plate LIX) does Chippendale warn against this: 'The Feet and Rails [i.e. frieze] are cut through; which gives it an airy Look; but will be too slight for Marble-Tops.' The smaller type of ornamental side table known as a console table which had been introduced from France earlier in the century remained strongly in fashion. The essential feature

Mahogany sideboard table in Gothic taste resembling a design (Plate LX) in the *Director* (1762). Victoria and Albert Museum, London.

of the console table was that it had its principal supports in front only, relying on the wall, against which it was placed, for back support. In this respect it can be distinguished from the pier table which stood squarely and independently on its own supports against the pier, the architectural term for the wall between windows. To help solve the structural problem of console tables their two front legs were given pronounced bow shapes, and much decoration was added to their friezes and stretchers. In fact these tables can claim to share with mirrors the distinction of being the most fanciful interpretations of Rococo taste. The *Director* designs for console tables show considerable overloading of carved decoration. None seems to have been executed, an indication no doubt that their intricacies may have been too much for the craftsmen of the time. They are certainly among the few examples of Chippendale's designs about which he is plainly unhappy.

The case is quite different with his other small tables. Since the end of the 17th century the English had become the greatest tea drinkers in Europe, and among the more attractive of Chippendale's pieces were his rectangular '**china tables**', so called because the tea things stood on them. The *Director* displayed several

Mahogany china table, the gallery and brackets pierced with foliage decoration. About 1755–1760.

patterns of Chinese frets for decorating the delicate little gallery which was fitted to the edge of the table to safeguard the precious china. There were also three designs for 'tea-kettle stands', two of box-like form, the other of the familiar 'pillar-and-claw' type, the current term for the tripod base supporting a shaft and circular top, complete again with a tiny pierced gallery. Small

27 **breakfast tables** were also fashionable. Breakfast was often taken upstairs in the bedroom, as it was a late meal among the leisured classes in Chippendale's time, and so breakfast tables were designed to match the rest of the bedroom furniture. The two varieties illustrated in the *Director* both had flaps, but while

27 one had a **lower shelf** enclosed by fretwork, the other had stretchers only beneath the top.

Chippendale paid great attention to library furniture, and indeed English craftsmen may claim credit for being among the first in Europe to develop pieces for use in this room. **Library**

26, 57 **tables** were predominantly of the open pedestal type, with kneehole and flanking drawers or cupboards. That this particular

Mahogany library table supplied by Chippendale to Nostell Priory in 1767 for £72 10s. Collection of Lord St Oswald, Nostell Priory, Yorkshire.

'Breakfast Tables.' Plate LIII, *Director* (1762). (See below)

Breakfast table in mahogany, with shelf enclosed by frets, based on a design (Plate LIII) in the *Director* (1762). About 1759. Collection of the Marquis of Bute, Dumfries House, Perthshire. (See above)

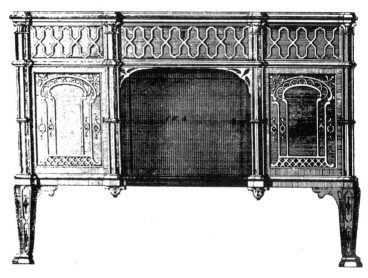

'Writing Table.' Plate LXXVI, *Director* (1762). (See below)

Mahogany writing table based on Plate LXXVI in the *Director* (1762). (See above)

type was fashionable is indicated by the fact that the number of their designs went up from six in the first edition of the *Director* to eleven in the third. They were inclined to be large pieces, their decoration varying from low relief frets on the frieze and pilasters to delicate Rococo carving on the cupboard doors. Five plates of

28   **writing tables** were also shown; there was much variety in the designs, some being straight-legged types with rectangular tops (sometimes with concave ends) and others pedestals with a superstructure of small cupboards, pigeon holes and drawers. Bookcases seem to have had a special interest for Chippendale. Fourteen designs were illustrated. Exact measurements were given, and on separate plates profiles of mouldings 'at large' were shown,

29   engraved with considerable detail. The **break-front** type was favoured, i.e. with a centre section flanked by recessed wings. Glazing bars were in various lattice forms and were particularly graceful. The architectural character of bookcases was very

Mahogany break-front bookcase supplied by Chippendale to Sir Lawrence Dundas in 1764 for £73. Collection of the Marquis of Zetland, Aske Hall, Yorkshire.

strongly stressed, and the pediment was given different forms—
16 triangular, broken and swan-necked. **Gothic bookcases** had a straight top across which ran a pierced fret of Gothic tracery, or else the cupboard doors had surmounting pointed arches and finials. In each case the glazing bars emphasised the style with cusped arches. All the bookcases (and some of the largest were fifteen feet wide, with five compartments) had solid bases, or cupboard bases with solid doors. The two-staged piece which
31 today is called a **bureau-bookcase** was known in Chippendale's times as the 'Desk and Bookcase'. The desk or bureau section had various forms (normally, of course, with the characteristic sloping writing top), such as a chest of drawers, or cupboard, in both these cases with bracket feet, or a shallower chest of drawers, described as a 'frame', on cabriole legs. A version of the desk and bookcase was called a 'Dressing Chest and Bookcase'; it had a lower stage composed of a knee-hole desk, and was designed for writing letters in the bedroom or dressing-room. All these combined pieces had their upper doors glazed with looking-glass. This was an expensive business as mirror glass was costly and normally had to be ordered by the cabinetmakers from the glassmakers. In practice it seems to have been more usual to enclose the shelves with solid wooden doors.

One apparently strange omission in the *Director* is any design for a dining-table. The reason for this was that since the 17th century the long, standing dining table had gone right out of fashion. It was altogether too clumsy. Instead two or three smaller tables were joined up when required and then, after a meal, dismantled and placed separately against the wall.

A number of designs for cabinets appeared in the *Director*, for the display of china or 'curiosities' (the collections of small but very valuable objects such as coins and jewels which were found in many rich households). China cabinets naturally called for decoration in the Chinese style, and had pagoda tops, fretted galleries, and low relief frets on the frieze, legs and brackets. Some china cabinets were quite small and were designed to hang on the wall.

For Rococo asymmetry in its freest expression, there was

The famous 'violin' bureau-bookcase in mahogany. About 1760. Attributed to Chippendale. Collection of the Earl of Pembroke, Wilton House, Wiltshire.

left 'Glass Frames.' Plate CLXXI, *Director* (1762). (See 14)

right Carved and gilt girandole, one of a pair. Probably supplied by Chippendale in 1760. Collection of the Earl of Harewood, Harewood House, Yorkshire.

nothing among the designs in the *Director* (except console tables)
14, 32   to match those for **mirror frames** and pier glasses. The high cost of mirror glass has been referred to, and it would seem that as pieces of this kind could only have been made for wealthy clients there was no point in sparing expense. They were essentially carvers' work. The frames, which were intended to be gilded, were covered with a tremendous profusion of swirling scrolls with which, in some instances, Chinese motifs were mixed. Such mirrors, in their prominent position on the wall, must have had an astonishing effect, not least for their marked contrast with the formal architectural frames of the Kent era. The same free expression was evident in the smaller wall mirrors with candle brackets
32   –the **girandoles** or wall lights. To all these mirror frames Chippendale's textual note, referring to the larger mirrors, can be extended: 'A skilled carver may, in the execution of this and the following designs, give full scope to his capacity.'

    Several designs for clock cases were illustrated in the *Director*. A number, not very happy ones, were for longcase ('grandfather') clocks. These tall cases, however, had not been so fashionable since about 1740, when the first signs of the Rococo phase were becoming apparent, as they did not lend themselves easily to the
33   new forms of decoration. The smaller **table clocks** or bracket

Mahogany table clock based on a design (Plate CLXV) in the *Director* (1762). Movement by Alexander Cumming. About 1765.

Mahogany shaving table supplied by Chippendale to Paxton House in the 1770s for £7 7s. Collection of Mrs H. Home Robertson, Paxton House, Berwickshire.

clocks were more successful, and in two illustrated in the *Director*, Chippendale neatly incorporated Chinese fretwork with touches of the Rococo. But the preference at the time was for cartel clocks which hung on the wall and had carved frames in full Rococo taste. A fine example 'fit for a Public Hall or an Assembly Room' was shown on Plate CLXVI, with four spring (i.e. table) clocks also in Rococo style.

It is impossible here to give a detailed description of the many other pieces which are illustrated in the *Director*. There are several modern reprints of the book which will repay close study. Among the smaller pieces may be mentioned **shaving tables**, basin stands and brackets. Beds perhaps merit a few further words. These were magnificent structures, complete with costly hangings. The *Director* included designs for Gothic, Chinese, dome, couch, state and field beds, as well as for bed pillars and cornices. One design (Plate XXXIX) had the note: 'a Bed which has been made for the Earls of Dumfries and Morton'. A famous example which has been associated with Chippendale is the **Chinese bed**, with latticework back and pagoda tester, japanned red and green, formerly at Badminton House, now in the Victoria and Albert Museum, London. However, it is now almost certain that this bed was supplied by Linnell.

The success of the *Director* was infectious, for it was quickly followed by several similar pattern books. One close imitator was the *Universal System of Household Furniture*, published between 1759 and 1762 by the well known London firm of Ince & Mayhew (Ince was a subscriber to the *Director*). This book had over 300 designs and explanatory notes in both English and French, with the obvious intention of trying to get into the French market. (A French edition of the *Director* was also published in 1762.) In 1760 a group of leading designers calling themselves a Society of Upholsterers, Cabinet-Makers, etc., issued *Household Furniture in Genteel Taste for the Year 1760*. Contributors included Chippendale, Ince & Mayhew, Robert Manwaring, and probably Thomas Johnson. Manwaring was also responsible for two specialist books, *The Cabinet and Chair-Maker's Real Friend and Companion* (1765) and *The Chair-Maker's Guide* (1766).

Bedstead of japanned wood with gilt ornament, formerly in the Chinese Bedroom, Badminton House, Gloucestershire. About 1754. Probably by Linnell. Victoria and Albert Museum, London.

Chippendale's Patrons

The success of the *Director* inevitably raises the question of the number of pieces based on the designs in the book which can be actually traced to Chippendale's workshop. There are many such surviving 'book pieces', but we know enough now, of course, not to fall into the trap of giving Chippendale the credit for all of them. The whole matter of authentic Chippendale pieces rests essentially on documentary evidence. Where bills from the firm survive and can be clearly related to furniture, Chippendale's authorship is beyond question. But this happy state of affairs seldom exists. Only a very few houses have preserved both bills and furniture, and even where bills have survived, the description of the piece may be so terse as to render positive identification impossible. This particularly applies to smaller pieces which can be described in a word or two. A number of houses have documentary evidence other than bills (household accounts, for instance, or receipts from the firm) which refer briefly to Chippendale. Sometimes the amount paid to him is recorded without details. If the house concerned retains some *Director* style furniture, there is a good case that Chippendale supplied at least some of it.

Once a piece has been positively identified by a bill, its construction and decoration can be thoroughly examined and may serve to establish the authenticity of undocumented pieces. It is becoming clear, as more and more pieces by Chippendale and his contemporaries are being identified, that the leading craftsmen of the time, like artists, architects and others, developed a style of their own, and that this stylistic test, if applied with caution and with reference to all available evidence, can be, within these limits, a generally reliable guide. A somewhat different problem arises when furniture based on *Director* designs is found in a house of a subscriber to the book. Can he be assumed to have been also a patron of Chippendale? If one regards this as a probability, and the furniture is of good quality, then there is a strong case for attribution.

At this point a brief summary may usefully be made of the houses (with the dates of documents and other evidence, and the names of the owners concerned) with which Chippendale is

'Cloaths Press' supplied by Chippendale to Paxton House in 1774 for £12 12s. Collection of Mrs H. Home Robertson, Paxton House, Berwickshire.

definitely known to have had business dealings. In many cases the connection occurs after 1765, when the Rococo was going out of fashion, and more will be said about this later. Collections of bills are extant for furniture at Nostell Priory, Yorkshire (Sir Rowland Winn, 1766–1771); Harewood House, Yorkshire (Edwin Lascelles, later Lord Harewood, 1772–1775); Burton Constable, Yorkshire (Sir William Constable, 1767–1779, the bills including furnishings for Sir William's house in London); Mersham-le-Hatch, Kent (Sir Edward Knatchbull, 1767–1778); Dumfries House, Ayrshire (Earl of Dumfries, 1759 and 1766); and Paxton House, Berwickshire (Ninian Home, 1774). Letters between Chippendale and the owners have survived at Nostell Priory and Mersham-le-Hatch. There are also bills for work executed for Sir Lawrence Dundas between 1763 and 1766 which do not specify which of his two houses, Moor Park, Hertfordshire, and 19 Arlington Street, London, was the destination of the furniture. In the Victoria and Albert Museum there are bills (1771–1772) for the furnishing by Chippendale of David Garrick's house, 5 The Adelphi, London. A unique inventory (probably

Set of shelves supplied by Chippendale to Paxton House in 1774 for 15s. Collection of Mrs. H. Home Robertson, Paxton House, Berwickshire.

dated 1779–1780) of furniture supplied by Chippendale in the 1770s to Sir Richard Worsley at Appuldurcombe Park, Isle of Wight, is also extant. All the above records provide valuable information even though they are by no means as complete as one would wish.

The names of houses and their owners which have much briefer records of Chippendale, usually a bill or two, or receipts from him, or a note of payment to him, are as follows: Ampton Hall, Suffolk, and Pall Mall, London (notebook of James Calthorpe, 1758); Sir Robert Burdett, Bramcote, Warwickshire, and Foremark Hall, Derbyshire (payments, 1766 and 1769); Blair Castle, Perthshire (bills to the Duke of Atholl, 1768); James Buller, Downes, Devon, and Morval, Cornwall (bill, 1757); Christ Church, Oxford (bill for library stools, 1764); Kenwood, Middlesex (bill, 1769); Lansdowne House, London (payments by Lord Shelburne, 1770 and 1772); Melbourne House, Piccadilly, London (Sir William Chambers's notebooks, 1773); Duke of Portland (bill for Welbeck Abbey or London house, 1766); Rousham, Oxfordshire (Sir Charles Cottrell, daybook note, 1764); Saltram House,

Giltwood candle stand, one of a pair, supplied by Chippendale to the Duke of Atholl in 1758. Collection of the Duke of Atholl, Blair Castle, Perthshire.

Devon (James Parker, account books, 1771–1772); Sandon Hall, Staffordshire (Lord Harrowby, steward's book, 1766 and 1777); Temple Newsam House, Leeds (Lord Irwin, small bill, 1774); Wilton House, Wiltshire (Earl of Pembroke, receipts, 1765–1791); 26 Soho Square, London (Sir William Robinson, bill, 1759–1760); Boynton Hall, Yorkshire (Sir George Strickland's account book, 1767); Denton Park, Yorkshire (Sir James Ibbotson, undated bill, about 1776); Audley End, Essex (Sir John Griffin Griffin, bill, 1774).

Dressing table in carved mahogany, based on a design in the *Director* (1762). Probably by Chippendale. Formerly at Kimbolton Castle, Huntingdonshire. Private collection.

Commode inlaid with various woods and mounted with ormolu. Attributed to Chippendale on stylistic grounds. About 1770. Renishaw Hall, Derbyshire.

Chippendale's part in the bankruptcy proceedings in 1772 of Madame Cornelys of Carlisle House, Soho Square, London, prove that he sold some furniture to her. 'Book pieces' and subscribers to the *Director* are linked at Alnwick, Northumberland (Earl, later Duke, of Northumberland, to whom the first edition of the *Director* was dedicated); Arundel, Sussex (Duke of Norfolk); Badminton House, Gloucestershire (Duke of Beaufort); and St Giles's House, Dorset (Countess of Shaftesbury). There are strong claims that Chippendale records, now lost, formerly existed at Langley Park, Norfolk, and Abbs House, County Durham. Notes to the plates in the third edition of the *Director* refer to designs carried out for Lord Pembroke (Plate XLVI) and, as already noted, for the Earls of Dumfries and Morton (Plate XXXIX). Another note (Plate LII, a lady's dressing table) states that two examples 'have been made of Rose-Wood from this Design', and this reference has linked Chippendale's name with Kimbolton Castle, Huntingdonshire (Duke of Manchester) which formerly had a **dressing table** based on this plate. Chippendale has also been associated

Cabinet with ormolu mounts and veneered with satinwood and inlaid with various woods. About 1770–1775. Attributed to Chippendale on stylistic grounds. Formerly at Panshanger, Hertfordshire. Collection of Viscountess Gage, Firle Place, Sussex.

Pole screen with mahogany pillar and claw. Panel of Fulham tapestry. Supplied by Chippendale to Dumfries House in 1759 for £4 4s. Collection of the Marquis of Bute, Dumfries House, Ayrshire.

through 'book pieces' (but so far without any confirmatory evidence) with **Raynham**, Norfolk (Captain Townshend); Corsham Court, Wiltshire (Paul Methuen); Coombe Abbey, Warwickshire (Lord Craven); and Crichel, Dorset (Sir William Napier). Stylistic evidence similarly associates him, in the later Neoclassical phase, with **Renishaw Hall**, Derbyshire, and **Panshanger**, Hertfordshire.

22
41
42

The above list of houses shows the wide geographical extent of Chippendale's commissions, in which his native Yorkshire figured prominently, as well as the quality of his clients. As Chippendale is known to have visited many of these houses in the course of his work, the physical strain involved in travelling, in the conditions of the 18th century, must have been very considerable.

In spite of the accumulating documentary material concerning Chippendale's work, there is far less authenticated furniture from his workshop in the *Director* style than in the later Neoclassical. The most famous piece of the Rococo period which has so far been positively identified is actually a late example and shows signs of the nascent Neo-classicism. This is the famous

26 **library table** supplied to Sir Rowland Winn at Nostell Priory, described in the bill in 1767 thus:

> ... a large mahogany library table of very fine wood with doors on each side of the bottom part and drawers within on one side and partitions on the other, with terms of ditto carv'd and ornamented with Lions' heads and paws with carv'd ovals in the pannels of the doors and the top cover'd with black leather ... ... £72 10s. 0d.

This table has carving of superb quality. Almost certainly Chippendale supplied other furniture at Nostell in the *Director* tradition, including a break-front bookcase with foliated Gothic glazing bars, a pair of hanging shelves, a commode with ormolu mounts, a mahogany writing table with a fretted upper stage, a set of dining-room chairs and a knee-hole cabinet. There are other pieces which have been clearly identified – Nostell in fact has the largest known collection of documented Chippendale furniture – but they are all post-Rococo. Dumfries House has a number of documented pieces much closer to the *Director* phase, dating from 1759, and including a rosewood bookcase with gilt enrichments, a pair of card tables, fourteen 'elbow chairs' and two large sofas matching the card tables, a breakfast table, a butler's tray,

42 three **pole (or fire) screens** with Fulham tapestry panels, and a pair of carved and gilt girandoles. A fine set of chairs and a picture frame at Abbs House are in full Rococo taste and are almost certainly by Chippendale, for a very strong tradition exists concerning his accounts, though these are now missing. A secrétaire-bookcase of 1764 attested by a Chippendale bill for the price of £26 is now at Aske Hall, Yorkshire, the seat of the Marquess of Zetland, direct descendant of Sir Lawrence Dundas to whom Chippendale's bills were originally submitted. Also at

29 Aske Hall are a **bookcase** and library table from Chippendale's workshop. He supplied Sir Lawrence Dundas in 1766 with '10 Large French Arm Chairs very richly carv'd and gilt in Burnish'd Gold' for £130, together with three matching sofas for £105. This suite in Rococo taste has been sold and is now in Birr Castle, Ireland. It should not be confused with the very similar suite of 1765 which (as shown on page 55) was made by Chippendale to

43

left Medal cabinet of carved mahogany, altered by William Vile for George III in 1761. Victoria and Albert Museum. London.

below Mahogany bookcase made by William Vile for Queen Charlotte in 1762. Royal Collection.

Adam's design, also for Sir Lawrence. The long record of receipts from Chippendale to the Earl of Pembroke make it almost certain that many of the pieces in *Director* tradition at Wilton House came from his workshop. This has always been considered the case with the famous **'violin' bookcase** at Wilton which is based on Plates LXXXVII and XCII in the *Director*. En suite with this bookcase are a pair of break-front bookcases which are obviously from the same source.

31

Mention has already been made of the fact that Chippendale had gifted contemporaries. Outstanding among them was William Vile who with his partner, John Cobb, served George III at the beginning of his reign after having previously been in the service of the Dowager Princess of Wales at Windsor Castle. Some of the magnificent furniture which Vile supplied to the royal households (all fully documented and still in royal possession) are among the greatest masterpieces of English furniture. They include a jewel-cabinet and bureau-cabinet (both 1761) and a **bookcase** of architectural form (1762) made for Queen Charlotte, and a pair of **medal cabinets** adapted for George III (1761). The carving on these pieces is unsurpassed in the whole history of English furniture, and indeed the bookcase is perhaps the finest example of case furniture ever made in England. For work in the Rococo style, Vile must be ranked superior to Chippendale. Cobb continued the firm's business (in St Martin's Lane) after Vile's retirement in 1764 and specialised in the inlaid furniture which was fashionable in the Neo-classical period.

44
44

Another rival to Chippendale was Pierre Langlois of Tottenham Court Road, who from about 1760 was making furniture, particularly commodes in the French manner. He was presumably a French immigrant, but his background remains very obscure, and although his identified work is of high quality there is a tendency today to attribute furniture to him on insufficient evidence. Another prominent firm were Ince & Mayhew, already noted as publishers of the *Universal System*. Finally there was Thomas Johnson, designer and carver, whose published books of designs and attributed carvings of mirrors, girandoles, chimneypieces, etc. reveal a lively interpretation of the Rococo.

Mahogany chair with profuse Rococo carving. Made in Philadelphia. H. F. du Pont Winterthur Museum, Delaware.

The Chippendale style enjoyed a great vogue abroad. Ever since the end of the 17th century England had been exporting to her colonies and to many parts of Europe increasing quantities of furniture which was prized for its elegance and sound craftsmanship and also served as models for colonial and foreign craftsmen to imitate in their own versions. Now the *Director* was also available for export. Visitors to museums overseas will often come across charming translations of *Director* pieces. Some brief references to chairs may serve here to exemplify some of these adaptations. 'American Chippendale' furniture was made throughout the colonies, with local variations, from about 1760 to 1780. In the important furniture centre of **Philadel-**
46 **phia**, chairs were particularly noted for their profuse Rococo carving, but some of them, like those attributed to **Benjamin**
47 **Randolph**, kept more closely to the *Director* by employing Gothic tracery on the splat and French scroll feet (the latter were very rarely used on American furniture, which favoured the claw-and-ball).

Both northern and southern Europe felt the influence of the

One of six mahogany chairs probably made by Benjamin Randolph in about 1765–1780. Colonial Williamsburg, Virginia.

Director. One country with a national version of Chippendale's style was Portugal, England's close trading partner. '**Portuguese Chippendale' chairs** were often made of rosewood (from Portugal's colony, Brazil) which owing to its extreme hardness produced thinner structural members, including cabriole legs, than was the case with mahogany. Carving tended to be shallow and often took asymmetrical forms on the splat. Spain too, despite her colonial rivalry with England, imported much English furniture, and Chippendale inspired the splatwork of many **Spanish chairs** which otherwise had typical Spanish carving and gilding and were made of walnut or poplar. **Denmark** and Norway (then a joint kingdom) were also devotees of English furniture. In **Norway** the first impact of Chippendale's influence, about 1760, was to give an asymmetrical twist to the carved shell and foliage ornament which was found on the popular curvilinear chairs based on English early Georgian types. It was distinctly later that the full *Director* style gave Norwegian chairs their pierced splats and 'cupid's bow' crests. These were being widely imitated in the late 1780s.

left Mid 18th-century
Portuguese chair. Museu
Nacional de Arte Antiga,
Lisbon.

right Spanish mid 18th-century chair.
Museo de Artes Decorativas, Madrid.

below Unpainted beechwood chair made in
Denmark in 1767–1768 for the town hall of Altona
(Holstein). Kunstindustrimuseet, Copenhagen.

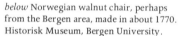

below Norwegian walnut chair, perhaps
from the Bergen area, made in about 1770.
Historisk Museum, Bergen University.

Neo-classicism

The success of the *Director* in England was relatively short-lived. 1762, the date of its third and final edition, marked the real limit of its influence, for already the Rococo was being superseded by a new style, Neo-classicism. There is controversy, still unresolved, whether this style originated in France or England. Whatever the truth, there is no doubt that it developed in England in a highly individualistic manner under the direction of one outstanding personality, Robert Adam, the Scottish architect who set up practice in London in 1758 with his three brothers (James, his chief assistant, John and William), and rapidly established his reputation in the 1760s. English architecture, interior decoration and crafts, fused together as never before, now entered upon perhaps the most brilliant phase in their history. Chippendale, the creator of one style, was destined to become one of the most gifted exponents of furniture in another. Neo-classicism marked a return to classical order after the wayward frolics of the Rococo, but it was classicism revived in a light and delicate form which captured much of the light-heartedness of its predecessor. It was an integral feature of the new style that everything about the house, outside and in, should conform to a unified decorative scheme. Until recently, it was always assumed that Adam, the designer in chief, must have designed all the furniture in his houses which conformed so admirably to his style. He certainly designed some pieces, for designs of furniture by him can be found in the great collection of his drawings preserved in the Soane Museum, London, and a number of his furniture designs have also survived in some of his houses.

But there is a considerable amount of furniture in the Adam style for which no drawings exist, and the former assumption that Adam did the designs and that these were subsequently lost by the cabinetmakers to whom they were sent for execution is no longer acceptable. The general pattern seems to be that Adam was responsible for the design of the furniture intended to stand against the wall of the rooms which he decorated, such as side-boards, side tables, commodes, pier glasses, pedestals, cabinets, etc., all of which would naturally form an essential part of the architect's treatment of the room. But for most other pieces the owner of the house would call in cabinetmakers who would design and make the furniture to fit the decorative scheme. This does not, of course, rule out discussion and co-operation between architect and furniture-maker.

There is now no doubt that Chippendale designed most of the furniture in Neo-classical style which his firm produced, and his success in turning from his own style, largely dependent on the carvers' skill, to a completely different one, in which mar-quetry was revived with great distinction, is a fine tribute to his outstanding ability as a designer. It also reflects the vast re-servoir of skilled craftsmanship in England that could promote this successful revival of marquetry when the technique had been out of fashion for half a century.

The 'electric power of this Revolution in Art', as Sir John Soane later described Adam's achievement, changed the whole appear-ance and decoration of furniture and interiors. Adam produced a 51 wonderful vocabulary of **classical decorative motifs**, including festoons of husks, honeysuckle, acanthus, paterae, vases, medal-lions, and rams' and satyrs' heads, applied in various ways. 41, 56, 61 **Marquetry**, reserved for the most magnificent furniture, was carried out in a variety of beautiful woods, usually with satin-wood, tulipwood, mahogany and harewood (i.e. stained syca-more) as a ground. Carved, gilt and painted decoration was also used, and another effective method was to set bright ormolu

Detail of gilt pine mirror, one of a pair, in Neo-classical style. Supplied by Chippendale to Burton Constable, Yorkshire, in 1774 for £52 the pair. Collection of Mr and Mrs J. Chichester Constable, Burton Constable, Yorkshire.

'Lyre back' armchair of carved mahogany, one of a set of six supplied by Chippendale in 1768 at a total cost of £36. Collection of Lord St Oswald, Nostell Priory, Yorkshire.

mounts against a dark mahogany background. Adam also devised some picturesque arrangements of furniture, exemplified in the matching pier glass and side table, and in the **sideboard com-**

58 **position** of table and wine cooler flanked by pedestal cupboards
52 with surmounting urns. Chairs acquired backs of **round**, oval,
51 heart, shield and **lyre shapes**, fluted seat rails, and straight tapered legs, round or square in section, often ending on plinth feet. These straight tapered legs, growing more slender in the 1770s, were an unmistakable feature of the new style, and were found, of course, on tables as well as on chairs.

Drawing by Chippendale of an armchair at Burton Constable. About 1775. Inscribed 'Chipindale' by Sir William Constable's steward. Collection of Mr and Mrs J. Chichester Constable, Burton Constable, Yorkshire.

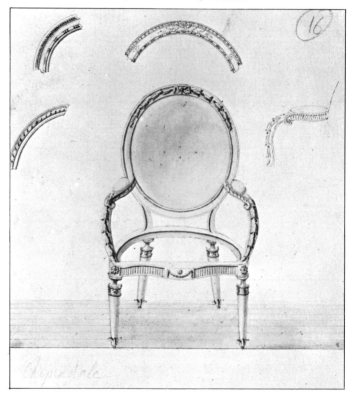

Proof that Chippendale did his own designs of furniture in the Adam style occurs in a letter he himself wrote to Sir Rowland Winn in July 1767:

'I have taken the liberty of informing you of the reason why I have not Call'd upon you at Nostell. As soon as I had got to Mr. Laselles and look'd over the whole of the house I found that I shou'd want a Many designs and knowing that I had time Enough I went to York to do them.'

52 At Burton Constable there are some **pen and wash drawings** for furniture and ornaments inscribed with the name 'Chipindale' in the hand of John Raines, Sir William Constable's steward. These are elegant designs, one of them showing a round-back armchair with fluted serpentine front seat rail and straight tapered legs in an attractive version of the new mode. The date of the drawings is about 1775, and they represent the kind of series of designs which Chippendale submitted to his clients after obtaining the commission for their furniture.

In 1773 a reference to Chippendale in the correspondence of Sir William Chambers, then engaged in building Melbourne House, Piccadilly, London, for Lord Melbourne, illustrates the consultation which normally took place between architect and cabinetmaker. Chippendale had been commissioned to supply the furniture and arrange it about the house. Chambers was deeply concerned that the disposition of the furniture should conform to his own decorative scheme, and he prevailed on Lord Melbourne to insist that Chippendale should submit his designs for Chambers's approval before carrying them out. Finally, Appuldurcombe Park gives us an example of the complete furnishing by Chippendale's firm in the Neo-classical style of a house with which Adam had no connection at all. The furniture has now dispersed, but the inventory of about 1779–1780 leaves no doubt about the preponderance of Neo-classical pieces. They included eight fine chairs in the library, 'Antique urn back, carved and inlaid', inset with a Wedgwood medallion in the top of the back, which are now at Brocklesby Park, Lincolnshire.

On the other hand, Chippendale is known to have made furniture specifically from Adam's designs. Note has already been

Giltwood chair, part of a suite, made by
Chippendale to a design by Robert Adam, in
1765, for Sir Lawrence Dundas. Victoria and
Albert Museum, London.

made of the chairs and sofas supplied by Chippendale to Sir Lawrence Dundas in 1766. Another invoice from Chippendale 54 to Dundas in July 1765 was for '7 large **Arm Chairs** exceeding Richly Carv'd in the Antick manner ... £160', and '4 large Sofas exceeding Rich to match the chairs ... £216'. Adam's design (for which he charged Dundas £5) for the sofas has survived and is dated 1764. This gilt suite, which was decidedly more expensive than Chippendale's own suite of about the same date, shows the interesting transitional stage between Rococo and Neoclassical, the latter being marked by the arabesques, sphinxes and honeysuckle carved on the seat rails and cresting. Only recently has this example of Adam-Chippendale co-operation come to light. The suite was formerly attributed to Samuel Norman, the royal cabinetmaker.

'Antique' or 'antick' is used by Chippendale in his accounts to describe a piece in the Adam style. For his masterpieces in this mode we have to turn to the accounts at Harewood House, where he was active between 1769 and 1777. His total bill in 1777 amounted to the considerable sum of £6839, but the surviving accounts date only from the end of 1772, and previous details, represented by a bill of £3025 (i.e. nearly half the total), are missing. Fortunately, one of the greatest triumphs of English cabinetmaking can be positively identified from the following entry of November 1773:

> A very large rich Commode with exceeding fine Antique Ornaments curiously inlaid with various fine woods, Drawers at each end and enclosed with foldg. Doors, with Diana and Minerva and their Emblems Curiously Inlaid and Engraved, a Cupboard in the middle part with a Cove Door, a Dressing Drawer in the Top part, the whole Elegantly Executed and Varnished, with many wrought Brass Antique Ornaments finely finished ... ... £86.

56 This '**Diana and Minerva**' **commode** alone would completely justify Chippendale's great reputation. Its price, £86, is the highest that he is known to have charged for a piece of case furniture (mirrors cost more because of the great expense of the glass), and it has been computed that it took three months' fulltime labour to

make. It is veneered with the finest West Indian satinwood, the festoons of husks are stained green, and the figures of the two goddesses on the doors are executed in coloured woods and ivory on a ground of ebony. The concave lunette ('cove door') in the centre, the concave ends and the top are all inlaid in the same superb fashion. The feet and pilasters are mounted in ormolu. The stylistic evidence of this commode surely gives Chippendale

41 also the credit for the outstanding but undocumented **commode** at Renishaw Hall, for both have strikingly corresponding decoration, feet and pilasters. Similarly, Chippendale can be credited

42 with the fine **cabinet** formerly at Panshanger (now at Firle Place, Sussex) though this is again undocumented.

Another famous Harewood piece, which attracted much attention in 1965 when it was acquired by Temple Newsam for 41,000

57 guineas, is the **library table**. This is not mentioned in the ac-

The famous 'Diana and Minerva' commode, of satinwood inlaid with various woods, supplied by Chippendale to Harewood House in 1773 for £86. Collection of the Earl of Harewood, Harewood House, Yorkshire.

counts, but the Harewood *Day Work Book* discloses that in 1772 Chippendale's foreman, William Reid, made dust covers for this table, following the custom of firms supplying such protective material for their expensive pieces. There is nothing whatever to connect Robert Adam with the design of any of the above furniture, even though it was so obviously influenced by his style. There are no designs or bills from Adam at Harewood, and no bills from any rival London firms. Thus the celebrated 58 **rosewood sideboard**, pair of pedestals and urns, and wine cooler at Harewood, with ormolu mounts in Neo-classical style, which have so often been regarded as an outstanding example of the Adam-Chippendale union is without question Chippendale's sole responsibility. His work in the 1770s placed English furniture in the same rank as the most important products of contemporary French cabinetmakers.

Library table of rosewood inlaid with various woods and mounted with ormolu. Probably supplied by Chippendale to Harewood House in about 1770 (he is known to have supplied its dust cover). Temple Newsam House, Leeds.

Sideboard table, pedestals, urns and wine cooler in rosewood mounted with ormolu. Probably supplied by Chippendale in about 1770–1775. Collection of the Earl of Harewood, Harewood House, Yorkshire.

Wardrobe, japanned in gold and silver on a green ground. Supplied by
Chippendale. About 1770. Collection of Lord St Oswald, Nostell Priory, Yorkshire.

It is impossible here to detail all of Chippendale's post-*Director* work. Further information can be found in the following: *The Journal of the Furniture History Society* (Vol. IV, 1968), for the complete Chippendale letters and accounts at Harewood, Nostell and Mersham-le-Hatch; Eileen Harris, *The Furniture of Robert Adam* (1963), for a full study of the Adam-Chippendale relationship; A. Coleridge, *Chippendale Furniture* (1968), for the *Director* period; and C. Musgrave, *Adam and Hepplewhite Furniture* (1966) for the later phase.

The accounts underline Chippendale's extraordinary versatility. At Nostell there is a remarkable **suite of japanned bedroom furniture** in green and gold, and other pieces demonstrate his

60-62

Commode, japanned in gold and silver on a green ground. Supplied by Chippendale. About 1770. Collection of Lord St Oswald, Nostell Priory, Yorkshire.

early efforts with the emergent Adam style. At Mersham-le-Hatch the supply of furniture was put into his hands after Adam had built and decorated the house, and though it lacked here the splendour of that at Harewood and Nostell it was of uniformly good quality and included many japanned and painted articles. The inlaid decoration of a side table at Mersham so closely

62 matches that of a beautiful **small commode** of unknown provenance as to denote the same maker, while the commode matches

Green japanned dressing table, probably by Chippendale. About 1770. Collection of Lord St Oswald, Nostell Priory, Yorkshire.

Commode table of about 1775, closely related to a chest of drawers at Syon House, Middlesex, and with frieze decoration identical with that on a side table at Mersham-le-Hatch, Kent. Attributed to Chippendale.

Mahogany bedside commode supplied by Chippendale to Paxton House in 1774 for £2 12s. 6d. Collection of Mrs H. Home Robertson, Paxton House, Berwickshire.

a chest of drawers at Syon House, Middlesex. It is perhaps this pursuit of clues provided by correspondence of decoration which will more than anything else identify Chippendale pieces in the future. Paxton House is particularly interesting because although the furnishings of the chief reception rooms are in advanced Neo-classical taste, as one would expect from the date of the accounts (1774), the bedroom furniture conforms to the *Director* period. In all his houses we are reminded of the great diversity of equipment which his shop was expected to provide. Upholstery included a whole range of materials – carpets, curtains, bed-clothes, mattresses, pillows, sunblinds and all sorts of hangings – as well as the normal fixed or loose covers of seat furniture.

63 Cheap **plain utility furniture** was often supplied. At Nostell, household equipment included three dozen meathooks (14s. 6d.) and a large elm chopping block (10s.) for the kitchen. The firm also carried out cleaning and repair work there, even such trifling matters as:

> Plaining over a Kitchen Table, mending a sash and putting a lock on a drawer ... ... 4s.

Acknowledgements

The illustration at the bottom of page 44 is reproduced by gracious permission of Her Majesty the Queen.

The publishers wish to express their thanks to Major Tom Ingram and the Editors of *Apollo* and *Connoisseur* for help with the illustrations, and to Mr Anthony Coleridge for lending illustrations reproduced in *Chippendale Furniture* (Faber and Faber 1968).

Photographs were supplied by the following: A.C. Cooper Ltd 29; *Country Life* 2, 27 bottom, 31, 33 top, 40, 41, 42, 58; S. Eost and P. MacDonald 35; Entwistle, Thorpe and Co., Manchester 26; Fine Art Engravers 32 right, 51 bottom, 60, 62 top; R.B. Fleming Ltd 4, 9, 19 bottom, 20, 21 top right, 22 top, 28 top, 32 left; Raymond Fortt 28 bottom; Christopher Gilbert, Temple Newsam House, Leeds, 19 top left, 51 top, 52, 57; Henry Francis du Pont Winterthur Museum 46; Historisk Museum, Bergen University 48 bottom right; Michael Holford 8; Hotspur Ltd 25, 62 bottom; Ideal Studio, Edinburgh 39; Kunstindustrimuseet, Copenhagen 48 bottom left; Lady Lever Art Gallery, Port Sunlight, Cheshire 10, 16; Metropolitan Museum of Art, New York 7; Museo de Artes Decoratives, Madrid 48 top right; Museu Nacional de Arte Antiga, Lisbon 48 top left; Philadelphia Museum of Art 22 bottom; Tom Scott, Edinburgh 12, 33 bottom, 37, 38, 63; H. Taylor, Bournemouth 14; Bertram Unné, Harrogate 56; Victoria and Albert Museum, London 19 top right, 21 bottom right and top left, 23, 24, 27 top, 44 top, 54; Delmore Wenzel, Colonial Williamsburg, Virginia 47.

COUNTRY LIFE COLLECTORS' GUIDES
Series editor Hugh Newbury
Series designer Ian Muggeridge

Published for Country Life Books by
THE HAMLYN PUBLISHING GROUP LIMITED
LONDON · NEW YORK · SYDNEY · TORONTO
Hamlyn House, Feltham, Middlesex, England

CHIPPENDALE
ISBN 0 600 43588 1
© The Hamlyn Publishing Group Limited 1971
Printed by Toppan Printing Co. (H.K.) Limited, Hong Kong